D0597417

Little Britches
★ RODEO ★

1698 BN-T 1-9-86 11:46   #8913

Little Britches
★ RODEO ★

by MURRAY TINKELMAN

★

With additional photographs by Ronni and Susan B. Tinkelman

★ *Greenwillow Books, New York* ★

8913

Siskiyou County
Schools Library

ACKNOWLEDGMENTS

Many thanks to Jim Chamley
and the National Little
Britches Rodeo Association
for their continued support

Copyright © 1985 by Murray Tinkelman
All rights reserved. No part of this
book may be reproduced or utilized in
any form or by any means, electronic or
mechanical, including photocopying,
recording or by any information storage
and retrieval system, without permission
in writing from the Publisher,
Greenwillow Books, a division
of William Morrow & Company, Inc.,
105 Madison Avenue, New York, N.Y. 10016.
Art direction and design
by Ava Weiss with Mina Greenstein

First Edition
10 9 8 7 6 5 4 3 2 1

Library of Congress
Cataloging in Publication Data
Tinkelman, Murray. Little Britches Rodeo.
Summary: Describes the rules and the events of
the annual Little Britches Rodeo
for boys and girls from eight
to eighteen-years-old.
1. Rodeos for children—Juvenile
literature. 2. Rodeos for children—
Rules—Juvenile literature.
[1. Rodeos]   I. Title.
GV1834.4.T56   1985   791'.8   84-13710
ISBN 0-688-04261-9
ISBN 0-688-04262-7 (lib. bdg.)

Printed in the United States of America

To Big Paul
and the Crotta Clan

EVENTS

A young cowboy practices calf
roping, using a bail of hay.

INTRODUCTION

Somewhere in the Southwest, sometime about 1883, a tiny crowd gathered to watch the first Professional Rodeo.

No one is really certain where or when it happened. We do know that on Saturday, August 29, 1952, in Littleton, Colorado, the first annual National Little Britches Rodeo began at 1:30 P.M. at the Arapahoe County Fairgrounds.

Little Britches has grown since that first rodeo in Colorado. There are now over one hundred rodeos a year. More than eighteen thousand young cowboy and cowgirl athletes ride to "win their world," and the silver trophy buckles sometimes seem bigger than the cowboys or cowgirls wearing them.

At the National Little Britches Rodeo Association Finals in Colorado Springs, Colorado, six hundred young cowboys and cowgirls compete in the same spirit that made that first 1880s rodeo cowboy bet, "I can ride anything with four legs."

"America's #1 Sport" includes cowboys and cowgirls from eight to eighteen years old. Little Britches Rodeo has four divisions: junior boys 8 to 13, senior boys 14 to 18, junior girls 8 to 13, and senior girls 14 to 18. Little Britches has all of the exciting events of Professional Rodeo.

There are five events for each of the four classes of cowboys and cowgirls, as well as two events where boys and girls compete together. This means that up to twenty-two different events may be run at a Little Britches Rodeo. It adds up to more than three times the action of a Professional Rodeo which generally runs about seven events.

There have been slight rule changes in some events and brand-new events have been added for the younger riders and ropers. But it's a real rodeo.

A plastic steer's head mounted on a bail of hay makes an ideal dummy for team roping practice.

The rodeo begins with all of the cowboys and cowgirls riding in the traditional grand entry.

As in Professional Rodeo, all cowboys and cowgirls ride with western saddles and must wear western hats, long-sleeved shirts with sleeves rolled down and tails tucked in, long pants, and boots.

The announcer then calls, "Bareback bronc riders, get ready! Your stock is in the chutes.

"It's the National Little Britches Rodeo Association Finals. Let's rodeo!" □

The flag bearer is a traditional part of the opening ceremonies.

Opposite: Aerial view of the bucking chutes, showing the broncs being readied for the first event.

Siskiyou County
Schools Library

Off to a good start, a senior bareback rider in perfect position.

BAREBACK BRONC RIDING

Senior Boys

Traditionally the opening event, bareback bronc riding, whether in Professional Rodeo or Little Britches, junior or senior, is the wildest and flashiest event in rodeo.

The cowboy rides without a saddle for eight seconds while holding on to the bareback rigging handhold with one gloved hand. The handhold must be made of leather or rawhide and looks much like a suitcase handle.

The bronc wears a soft pad under the rigging and a fleece-lined flank strap which causes him to kick higher and harder.

The "marking-out" rule requires the cowboy to have both spurs touching the horse, forward of the horse's shoulders, when the horse's front feet touch the ground on the first jump out of the chute. The cowboy then spurs high and hard for the rest of the ride.

Each of the two judges may award up to twenty-five points to the rider and twenty-five points to the animal for the one hundred point possible score.

The cowboy is disqualified for failing to "mark the horse out," touching himself or the horse with his free hand, or bucking off before the eight-second whistle. □

This "wreck" is not as bad as it looks. The cowboy was not injured.

Junior Boys

The same rules apply as in the senior boys' bareback bronc riding except that the horses are smaller, the time required to make a qualified ride is six seconds, and the "mark-out" rule is applied more leniently. ☐

A junior bareback rider gives his all.

A bronc in good form throws a junior rider.

This young cowboy has just been thrown, or gotten his "bell rung." Being shaken up is part of the learning process.

15

CALF ROPING

Senior Boys

Calf roping is one of the oldest events in rodeo. During the early days of the cattle business, cowboys had to rope calves from horseback for branding or doctoring.

In present-day rodeo the cowboy starts from behind a barrier rope, giving the calf a head start. The cowboy, on his highly trained horse, will race after the running calf, throw his rope, make the catch, dismount from his sliding horse, run along the rope and grab the lunging calf, throw the calf to the ground, tie three legs with his "piggen" string, and throw his hands into the air to signal that he is finished.

That's all there is to it, and if you can do it in under ten seconds, you're a cowboy.

Breaking the barrier adds a ten-second penalty to the time.

The calf must stay tied for five seconds, timed by the judges' stop watch. If the calf kicks free, the cowboy will receive "no time," that is, fail to qualify. □

A calf roper with the piggen string in his teeth waits for his turn.

*A young calf roper in
perfect form.*

A quick stop in a muddy arena to allow the calf to "pop the string."

BREAKAWAY CALF ROPING

Senior Girls · Junior Girls · Junior Boys

Breakaway roping is a modern rodeo event that is a variation of calf roping. In breakaway roping, time is flagged when the running calf pops the end of the lariat rope free from the saddle horn where it is tied with a piece of light string. A white flag must be attached to the rope at the saddle horn so the judge can tell when the rope breaks away. The roper is allowed to carry two ropes. If the first one misses the calf, the second may be thrown. As in all of the roping events breaking the barrier adds a ten-second penalty to the time.

This event is fine practice for junior boys who will move up to senior calf roping. □

The run is complete. The calf continues down the arena, trailing the rope with the white flag.

GOAT TYING

Senior Girls

 You must be an especially agile rider to win at this event.

The goat is tied to a stake with a ten-foot rope about fifty yards from the starting line. The cowgirl must ride from the starting line to the goat, dismount, and throw the goat to the ground. If the goat is already down, it must be brought to its feet and re-thrown. She then must tie three of its feet with her "piggen string." The goat must stay tied for five seconds, timed by the judges' stop watch. If the goat kicks free, the contestant will receive "no time."

The contestant will be disqualified if the horse touches the goat or the rope holding the goat, before or during dismounting. ☐

☞ *1 minute time limit*

Junior Boys

 The rules are the same as for senior girls. Like breakaway calf roping, this event is good practice for tying calves when the junior boys graduate to calf roping in the senior division. ☐

☞ *1 minute time limit*

*Opposite: A cowgirl makes a
flying dismount and heads for
the goat.*

*A cowgirl throws the goat to the ground and ties
three of his legs in good time.*

SADDLE-BRONC RIDING

Senior Boys

★ Saddle-bronc riding is rodeo's classic event and its oldest. It began at cattle roundups over a century ago when cowboys from neighboring ranches met and matched the riding skills of one top hand against the other.

In the rodeo arena today, the cowboy rides for eight seconds seated in his saddle while holding on to the "buck rein" with one hand. The saddle has no horn and is called an Association saddle. The cowboy must "mark" the bronc out of the chute by having both spurs touching the horse, forward of the shoulders, when the horse's front feet touch the ground on the first jump out of the chute. The cowboy then spurs smoothly backward and forward throughout the ride. A good bronc rider can make it look almost easy...it isn't.

The scoring is the same as bareback bronc riding and bull riding, with each of the two judges awarding up to twenty-five points to the rider and twenty-five points to the horse for the one hundred point possible score.

The cowboy is disqualified for failing to "mark the horse out," touching himself or the horse with his free hand, losing a stirrup, or bucking off before the eight-second whistle. □

A saddle-bronc rider carrying his association saddle.

A saddle-bronc rider is bucked off, or goes over the "dashboard."   **23**

A saddle-bronc contestant in mid-ride.

A steer wrestler makes a catch.

STEER WRESTLING

Senior Boys

 Steer wrestling requires practice, strength, and toughness, especially toughness.

The cowboy must catch a running steer by leaping off his horse and grabbing the steer by its head and horns, bringing it to a stop, and throwing it to the ground with its head and all four legs pointing in the same direction. If the steer is accidentally knocked down before being brought to a stop, it must be let up and then re-thrown.

The steer wrestler has a partner called a hazer. The hazer's job is to keep the steer running straight so that the steer wrestler can get a good jump.

The cowboy starts from behind a barrier rope and is penalized ten seconds if he breaks the barrier and starts after the steer too soon. The steers weigh between 450 and 750 pounds and it usually takes a good-sized cowboy to bring them down. □

☞ *1 minute time limit*

A steer wrestler strains to bring down a "rubberneck" steer.

Anything can happen during a steer-wrestling run.

A correct throw in a muddy arena.

BARREL RACING

Senior Girls · Junior Girls

This is the classic event of rodeo for girls.
The cloverleaf pattern around three barrels
is the only approved way to run this race. The cowgirl
may start at either the right or left barrel. When
starting at the right barrel there will be one right turn
and two left turns around the barrels, and when starting
on the left side, there will be one left turn and two right
turns. Knocking over a barrel adds a five-second penalty
to the time.

A cowgirl is disqualified if she does not follow the
cloverleaf pattern. □

*A junior barrel racer waits
for her turn.*

A junior barrel racer in a perfect turn.

A senior cowgirl makes a good turn and looks toward the next barrel.

Horse and rider lean in for a close turn around the barrel.

A senior cowgirl heads for the finish line.

A heeler sets the trap for the steer's hind feet.

TEAM ROPING

Senior Boys · Senior Girls

Cowboys still rope steers today as they did on the range one hundred years ago. Steers are much larger than calves and when they have to be branded or doctored it's a job for two people.

The team consists of a "header" and a "heeler." As in calf roping, the steer is given a head start and the header must not break the barrier rope when leaving the roping box. The header then ropes the seven hundred pound steer by the head, neck, or horns, takes a "dally," which is two turns of his rope, around the saddle horn, and turns the steer into position for the heeler to make his or her throw. The heeler catches both of the steer's hind legs and dallies, turning the horse to face both the steer and the other rider. The judges' flag signals time. A ten-second penalty is added to the team's time for breaking the barrier and a five-second penalty is added if the heeler catches only one hind leg.□

The end of the run. Team ropers face each other, waiting for the timer's flag.

DALLY RIBBON ROPING

Junior Boys · Junior Girls

★ This is a team event for junior cowboys and cowgirls. The team is made up of a roper and a runner and may consist of two girls, two boys, or a girl and a boy.

The roper ropes the calf, takes a dally around the saddle horn, and waits for the runner. The runner, who can be anywhere in the arena, must then run to the calf, which has a ribbon fastened to its tail with a rubber band, grab the ribbon, and run back to the roping box across the finish line. Time is flagged when the runner crosses the finish line.

Breaking the barrier adds a ten-second penalty to the time.

☞ *1 minute time limit. This includes the penalty for breaking the barrier.*

A young cowboy coils his rope.

Accidents will happen. A junior cowboy loses his footing as he reaches for the ribbon on the calf's tail.

GOAT TAIL TYING

Junior Girls

★ Goat tail tying is a race against the stop watch. The cowgirl must ride across the starting line, tie her horse to a "hitch," then go to the goat and tie a ribbon on its tail. The goat must be on its feet when tied. The cowgirl signals that she is finished tying the ribbon by raising both arms in the air. The ribbon must stay on for five seconds.

The cowgirl will be disqualified if she touches the ribbon again after signaling time, if her horse gets loose from its "hitch," or if the ribbon comes untied. □

☞ *1 minute time limit*

A junior cowgirl hitches her horse and runs for the goat.

A cowgirl ties a ribbon on the goat's tail while the timer looks on.

POLE BENDING

Senior Girls · Junior Girls

Pole Bending is another timed event.

The cowgirl may ride into the arena at the speed of her choice. She runs a course of six poles placed in a straight line, twenty feet apart, with the first pole twenty-one feet from the starting line. The rider may start either to the right or to the left of the first pole and run the rest of the pattern, weaving in and out of the alternate poles.

A five-second penalty will be added to the time for each pole knocked over.

The cowgirl is disqualified if she touches a pole with her hand or if she does not follow the course. ☐

A cowgirl makes her last turn and heads for the finish line.

A cowgirl and horse in fine form, weaving in and out of the poles.

FLAG RACE

Junior Boys

 Speed, skill, and horsemanship are combined in this event.

The course has two barrels spaced at least twenty-five feet apart, with a bucket of oats on each. A flag is stuck in the bucket on the barrel farthest away from the starting line. The cowboy is given a flag at the other end of the arena. He races across the starting line to the first or closest barrel and puts the flag in the bucket, races to the second barrel and retrieves that flag, then races back to the starting line. An experienced rider can do this on the dead run and finish the course in under ten seconds. Failure to carry the flag in the hand costs the cowboy a two-second penalty.

The cowboy will be disqualified for knocking over a bucket or barrel, for using the flag as a whip, or for not following the proper order of the race. □

☞ *1 minute time limit*

A junior flag racer approaches the bucket of oats.

At top speed he stretches to place the flag in the bucket of oats.

43

A junior cowgirl places a letter in the mailbox, the first obstacle in the trail course.

TRAIL COURSE

Senior Girls · Junior Girls

The cowgirl rides an obstacle course consisting of a bridge, a gate, a mailbox, brush panels, back-up barrels, and a jump.

The course for senior cowgirls must contain at least five of these obstacles, while the junior course must have at least four.

The cowgirl will be disqualified for knocking over any obstacle or for failing to complete the course.☐

☞ *1½ minute time limit*

A cowgirl backs her horse between two barrels.

A cowgirl opens and closes the gate.

A junior bullrider atop a high bucking bull.

BULL RIDING

Senior Boys

This last event of the rodeo does not seem very complicated—just stay on for eight seconds, that's all. The only problem is the bull. It may weigh as much as a ton and doesn't know or care that this is a Little Britches Rodeo. It is going to buck as hard as if a world champion professional were on its back.

The cowboy rides with one hand wrapped in a loose rope. The rope has a bell attached which annoys the bull and makes it buck harder.

Each of the two judges may award up to twenty-five points to the rider and twenty-five points to the bull for a possible one hundred points.

The cowboy is disqualified for touching himself or the bull with his free hand, for not being ready to mount his bull on time, or for bucking off before the eight-second whistle.

There is no "mark-out" rule in this event—bull riding is tough enough.

The clowns and bullfighters are the cowboy's best friends in the rodeo arena. Their job is to protect the cowboy after he jumps off or is bucked off the bull. A fallen cowboy may not be able to get out of the way of the charging bull and the clowns and bullfighters must distract the bull before it can reach the fallen rider. ☐

Junior Boys

The rules are the same as for the senior boys' bull riding except that the bulls are smaller, the ride is six seconds, and the bull rope is held but not wrapped around the rider's hand. ☐

He keeps his seat during a rough ride.

47

An early fall right out of the chutes.

A muddy cowboy retrieves his bull rope after a good ride.

A bull rider and bull in top form.

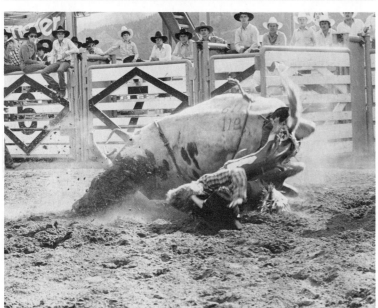

Siskiyou County
Schools Library

This sequence shows a bull rider as he avoids being pinned under a falling bull.

Young cowboys admire a friend's trophy buckle.

AFTERWORD

The finals are over. The last bull has been chased into the catch pen outside the arena. The stock contractor's wranglers have started to load the rough stock and cattle into trucks for the trip back to their home ranch.

Little Britches cowboy and cowgirl champions have won 488 trophy buckles, 34 saddles, and $26,000 scholarship money.

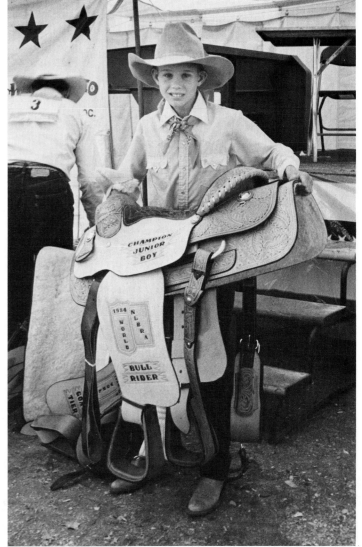

A junior bull rider proudly displays his new trophy saddle.

The young cowboys and cowgirls are shaking hands and saying goodbye to one another. They are about to be "going down the road." For some, that road will lead to high school, for others, college on a rodeo scholarship.

However, for that very special few, the road may eventually lead to the always hectic and exciting, but sometimes dangerous career on the Professional Rodeo circuit. □

Cowboys and cowgirls leave the arena after an evening performance.

GLOSSARY

Association Saddle · A hornless saddle built to Professional Rodeo specifications used for bronc riding.

Bareback Rigging · A piece of equipment cinched around the horse's belly that provides the bareback rider with a handhold.

Barrier · A rope stretched across the front of the box from which the roper's or steer wrestler's horse starts.

Breaking the Barrier · Riding through the barrier rope before it is released.

Buck Rein · A braided rein that is attached to a saddle bronc's halter. The rider must hold the rein in one hand, not change hands, and not wrap the rein around his hand.

Catch Pen · Holding area for cattle or rough stock.

Dally · Wrap the rope around the saddle horn after roping a steer.

Flagman · The rodeo official who signals the starting and stopping of the clock in timed events.

Flank Strap · A sheepskin-lined strap that encircles the bronc or bull behind the curve of its belly.

Hazer · The cowboy or cowgirl who rides along beside the steer, in the steer wrestling event, in order to keep the steer running in a straight line.

No Time · Failure to qualify in timed events, signaled by the flagman waving his flag from side to side.

Piggen String · A six-foot piece of rope used in tying the feet of the roped calf.

Rough Stock Events · The bareback bronc, saddle-bronc, and bull riding events.

Timed Events · Events that are judged by how much time has elapsed from start to finish.

Win the World · Win a championship.

Wrangler · Someone who handles livestock.

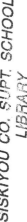

SISKIYOU CO. SUPT. SCHOOLS
LIBRARY
609 S. GOLD ST.
YREKA, CA 96097

89/3